Relationships
Are Forever

Relationships Are Forever

Once Born, One Cannot Be Unborn

Cal Hunter

WestBow
PRESS
A DIVISION OF THOMAS NELSON

WestBow Press books may be ordered through
booksellers or by contacting:

WestBow Press
A Division of Thomas Nelson
1663 Liberty Drive
Bloomington, IN 47403
www.westbowpress.com
1-(866) 928-1240

ISBN: 978-1-4497-5988-9 (sc)
ISBN: 978-1-4497-5989-6 (e)

Library of Congress Control Number: 2012912679

Printed in the United States of America

WestBow Press rev. date: 7/20/2012

Contents

Introduction

Thou hast made us for Thyself,
O' Lord, and our hearts are restless
'til they rest in thee.
-- Augustine

I had two major objectives in writing this book. First and foremost, I wanted to impart a deeper understanding of just who and what we Christian are; not what we ought to be, but according to the Holy Scriptures, who we actually are.

Second, I wanted to instill a greater recognition of the security of believers. Nothing renders us more sterile and impotent in our daily Christian lives than does the loss of the assurance of our salvation.

A greater understanding of the indestructible, eternal relationship we have with our heavenly Father deepens our faith and empowers us to lead more obedient and productive lives.

My earnest prayer is that you will experience these blessings in your walk with Jesus.

Chapter I
A Major Misconception

Several years ago when I was Director of Missions for Northwestern Oklahoma Baptist Association, I overheard two college- educated, seminary-trained pastors discussing whether or not a certain deacon could truly be a Christian and have committed the heinous sin he obviously was guilty of committing.

I have often recalled that incident and have come to the conclusion that if highly educated, trained pastors have such a limited knowledge of a true Christian, then certainly numerous lay people have that same problem.

Over the many years I have served in the ministry, I have often heard preachers and laymen alike argue that there are some sins a Christian cannot commit—not if he is truly born again.

Frankly, I believe the only sin a Christian *cannot* commit is the unpardonable sin in Matthew 12:31-32. Scholars seem to agree that whatever else may be included in this unforgiveable sin, it must surely include a conscious, willful, obstinate, determined refusal to accept God's offer of salvation through our Lord Jesus Christ. Because the born-again Christian has already received Jesus Christ as savior, it is impossible for him to commit the unpardonable sin.

The Holy Bible is replete with accounts of the sins of many biblical saints. Abraham, an Old Testament patriarch, lied when it became dangerous for him to admit Sarah was his wife. Noah got drunk. Moses committed murder. David was guilty of covetousness, adultery, and murder.

In the New Testament, the apostle Peter denied his relationship with Jesus and even cursed in an effort to convince Jesus' tormentors he was not one of His disciples. Too, the apostle Paul claimed he was chief of sinners.

I do not believe any other person, living or dead, lived a more perfect Christian life than did the apostle Paul; yet he wrote, "This is a faithful saying and worthy of all acceptance, that Christ Jesus came into the world to save sinners, of whom *I am chief*" (1 Timothy 1:15).[1]

Note the tense of the verb: *am,* not *was,* but *am. Robertson's Word Pictures in the New Testament* points out that the verb used here in the original Greek is not **hn** (I was), but **eimi** (I am). Robertson said it is not easy to think of anyone like St. Paul penning these words.

Over the many years I have served in the ministry, I have had occasion to counsel and advise numerous people, young and old alike. Long ago I noticed a strange phenomenon: those who laid no claim to being a Christian consistently indicated they felt as good as anyone who went to church. Conversely, I noticed that those who were

---

1   All scripture quoted from the New King James Version of the Bible.

exemplary Christians, consistently faithful in church, like the apostle Paul felt they were the worst sinners.

I have also heard many argue that when God saved them, He changed their "want to's." I agree this is partially true. I believe most who become Christians do lose some of their sinful desires they once had. I once heard a young preacher remark that after he became a Christian, he realized some of the things he previously thought brought him good times only brought him headaches.

I do believe that every born-again Christian has his own individual propensities to sin, a trait which Satan uses in an attempt to draw us away from following Christ.

The truth is temptations are essential to building Christian character. Every time we resist temptation, our faith is strengthened and our resolve to be faithful and obedient disciples brings peace and happiness in our soul. It is important to realize that mere temptation to sin is not a sin. Only when we give in to temptation have we actually sinned.

Former President Jimmy Carter once stated publicly that he had committed adultery many times because he could not help but note the sexual attraction of beautiful women. In fact, it is likely that most men cannot help but notice the sexual attributes of beautiful women. Jimmy Carter was a brilliant man. He held a Ph.D. in Nuclear Physics, commanded a nuclear submarine in the U.S. Navy, and was elected to the highest office in the United States, but Jimmy Carter was certainly no theologian.

I would like to inform President Carter that it is not a sin to take note of the sexual attraction of women who are so obviously endowed with such attributes.

Perhaps, however, it should be emphasized here that if a woman dresses with the intent of tempting a man into sin, it would be wrong for her to do so. On the other hand, if a man views such an attractive woman with lust in his heart, he is already sinning against God. The Bible teaches the following: if you would, if you could, then you already have!

I certainly do not want to sound like a prim paragon of virtue because I also have physical weaknesses. To illustrate my point: in all honesty, I have to admit at times I have been tempted to visit a porn site on the Internet, but I can honestly say that I have never one time visited a porn site. I would be a liar, however, if I claimed I had never been tempted to do so. I knew if I ever visited such a site one time, I would likely be unable to keep from doing it again and again, for such is the dynamic allure of temptation.

An excellent illustration of our proclivity to sin is seen in deep sea divers who experience a condition referred to as "Rapture of the Deep," a form of narcosis. Professional divers are carefully trained in the risks and means to prevent this hazardous condition from occurring. Narcosis may develop when diving at great depths, for the greater the depth, the greater the risk. Symptoms of narcosis are similar to the effects of alcohol consumption. Indeed, if the diver fails to recognize the on-coming symptoms, he experiences an intense sense of euphoria and becomes so enthralled with the surrounding beauty that he reaches a point from which he is incapable of turning back and continues until death ensures.

One of the strongest temptations to sin confronting mankind is our sexual drive. Scientists inform us that our sex drive is one of the strongest desires in human nature. Is it any wonder that our powerful sex drive enables one of Satan's greatest tools to lead us astray from faithful, loving obedience to our heavenly Father?

A major curse of sex outside of marriage is that it offers no satiety value. Satiety is the pleasant sense of utter satisfaction with one's pursuits. For instance, to insure a greater satiety value to a meal, dieticians recommend some form of sweet dessert at the conclusion of a feast. This addition greatly adds satiety value, a sense of profound satisfaction with the meal we have just devoured.

Illicit sex does not offer any degree of satiety value. Consequently, the drive for further illicit sexual adventure ensues, yet never produces any sense of lasting, warm, loving, satisfaction, i.e., satiety value.

How wonderful it would have been if God had indeed taken away all our sinful desires when He saved us, but He did not; however, His Word provides us with a broad and comprehensive understanding of the very nature of temptation and sin:

> Let no man say when he is tempted, 'I am tempted by God': for God cannot be tempted with evil, nor does He Himself tempt anyone. But every one is tempted when he is drawn away by his own desires and enticed. Then, when desire has

conceived, it gives birth to sin; and sin, when it is full-grown, brings forth death (James 1:13-16).

We learn from the above passage of Scripture:

First: "…nor does He tempt anyone." God never tempts anyone to sin!

Second: "…every one is tempted." We all have a sinful nature that tempts us to sin. It would even be risky and dangerous for us to pretend this was not true.

The Bible clearly states that "…e**very** man is tempted." Other Scriptures verify that statement: Romans 3:10, "There is none righteous, no not one…"; Romans 3:23, "…all have sinned and fall short of the glory of God…";
1 John 1:8,9, "If we say we have no sin, we deceive ourselves and the truth is not in us. If we confess our sin, He is faithful and just to forgive us our sins and to cleanse us from all unrighteousness."

Third: "…drawn away by his own desires." It is the things for which we lust, the things we desperately want but know we should not have, and when we give in to those desires, it causes us to commit sin.

Fourth: "...then when desire has conceived, it gives birth to sin." What a powerful statement: desire, if unrestrained, results in an illegitimate birth: sin."

Fifth: "...and sin, when it is fully grown, brings forth death." Romans 6:23 warns us "...the wages of sin is death, but the gift of God is eternal life in Christ Jesus our Lord."

To borrow a well-worn phrase, the "bottom line" is we have a sin problem which only God Himself can provide the cure.

Chapter II
What Is A Christian?

Over the years, I have asked folk in churches I pastored: "Just what is a Christian?" The various answers have been legion. Clearly, most people, including mature Christians, often lack a proper understanding of who and what we Christians are.

Some of the answers I have heard include the following:

"Someone who believes in Jesus."

"Someone who has been baptized."

"Someone who has joined the church."

"Someone who walks with Jesus."

All the above are, in fact, some of the characteristics of one who is a true Christian. On the whole, the best and most accurate definition of a Christian is simple and unequivocal: he is a **CHILD OF GOD!** This is not a rhetorical statement but a statement of fact! How on earth does one become a child of God?

A multitude of varying opinions exist on what is required of one in becoming a Christian. No other passage in Holy Scripture gives us more comprehensive, detailed information regarding this most important matter on earth than does the third chapter of the Gospel of John

In the third chapter of his Gospel, John tells us of a prominent citizen in Israel, Nicodemus, a Pharisee and a ruler of the Jews, who came to Jesus by night. Many explanations have been offered to explain why Nicodemus came at night rather than by day. Some have suggested he came by night to avoid others knowing he wished to speak with Jesus. Others have suggested he was too occupied in the daytime.

Regardless of why he came by night, the passage strongly implies that Nicodemus had heard of the many wonderful things Jesus had done. He had obviously heard stories of Jesus having healed all manner of sickness and infirmities, because the first words out of his mouth were "Rabbi (teacher), we know that You are a Teacher come from God; for no man can do these signs that You do unless God is with him" (v.2). Then, "Jesus answered and said to him, 'Most assuredly, I say to you, unless one is born again he cannot *see* the Kingdom of God'" (v.3). [Emphasis added.]

Since Jesus, being God in human flesh, knew what was on Nicodemus' mind, He proceeds to give an answer to Nicodemus' question even before it is asked.

What did Jesus mean by saying that one who has not experienced a second birth cannot even *see* the Kingdom of God? Nicodemus is confused and asks, "How can a man be born when he is old?" (v.4).

This reaction is typical of those who have never experienced the second birth. The reason for such response is obvious. The person who has not experienced the second birth is totally incapable of understanding the nature of the second birth *until* one has experienced it.

A classic example might be that student airplane pilots cannot possibly comprehend the "feeling" one must experience in landing an airplane until he has actually experienced it.

As a pilot approaches the runway, he gradually reduces power to slow the speed of the plane. Holding it a few feet above the runway, he continues to throttle back further to slow the plane more until he has slowed the aircraft down enough to pull further back gently on the yoke. At that time, the aircraft does not go back up but slowly, gently settles down on the runway. That's why it is often said that pilots must be able to fly an airplane by the seat of their pants.

It might be possible for a student pilot to learn how to fly and navigate an airplane in flight with nothing more than a flight simulator, but, a flight simulator can never create that "feeling" a pilot must have in order to get an airplane safely back on ground. He can only learn that "feeling" by actually experiencing it!

In 1 Corinthians 2:14, we read, "...the natural man does not receive the things of the Spirit of God for they are *foolishness* to him; nor can he know them, *because they are spiritually discerned.*" [Emphasis added.]

I can recall many times I have heard new believers cry out in exultation, "Oh! Why didn't I do this a long time ago? This is so wonderful; I feel so happy!" Now that they fully comprehend it, they cannot understand why they had not been able to do so earlier.

Nicodemus does not understand. He asks, "How can a man be born when he is old? Can he enter a second time into his mother's womb and be born?" (v.4).

People who have not yet experienced the second birth are as mystified today as they were 2,000 years ago when considering the second birth. Until one has experienced the second birth, these things remain cloudy and impossible to comprehend and may indeed appear to be foolishness.

In verse 5, "Jesus answered, 'Most assuredly, I say to you, unless one is born of water and of the spirit, he cannot enter the kingdom of God.'"

What did Jesus mean by "born of water?" No other theological question in all of history has resulted in a greater division of Christendom. It would not be far off to estimate that all Christendom is equally divided over the issue of whether "water" here refers to baptism or not.

Many scholars have maintained that Jesus was obviously speaking of baptism. Likewise, many denominations proclaim that while baptism is an ordinance that publicly proclaims our salvation experience, the rite of baptism plays no role in completing our salvation experience.

Chapter III
A Simple Explanation

I believe the answer to this question is pure and simple. Is Jesus God? If Jesus is truly God in every sense of the word, then I would like to suggest that when Jesus spoke these words to Nicodemus, He most assuredly knew there would be much confusion and that many would wonder why Jesus did not clarify the issue further. He is God and He did clarify the issue! With all that is within me, I want to assert unequivocally that Jesus is fully God, and being God, He was able to foresee that for thousands of years men would disagree, often vehemently, over what Jesus meant by "born of water."

I have often wondered what would happen if someone were willing to be saved, but no water was available. What if he died while waiting on water?

Let me put forth a hypothetical situation that could become reality. Suppose a young man who is a preacher's son learns to fly. He dearly loves to fly. For some reason he dreams of flying solo across the Sahara Desert. Ultimately, he realizes his dream and halfway across the territory, his plane develops engine problems and crash-lands in the desert sand. Critically wounded, he realizes he has no hope of getting help from any source and knows that shortly he will die. Although he is a preacher's son, he is not a Christian. All his life he has refused the invitation to become a born-again Christian. Now, knowing he is about to die, he desperately wants to be made right with his God. In agony, he cries out to God for God to save him, but there is no water, and there is no one to baptize him. Does this passage of Scripture in John 3:1-7 render it impossible for one to go to heaven simply because he has not been baptized? Ironically, this passage has caused much confusion and division among believers.

That is precisely why Jesus gave us the next verse: "That which is born of the flesh is flesh, and that which is born of the Spirit is spirit" (v.6). [Emphasis added.] Please take note: no water is mentioned here. Why? Because in verse 5, Jesus was referring to the natural, physical birth of a child as the "water birth."

As a physician, I have delivered babies. Everyone since the advent of Adam and Eve who has observed the natural birth of a baby has taken note of the watery delivery.

When a child is conceived, it is enveloped by the amniotic sac filled with water. This sac provides a soft, safe cushioning for the baby's comfort and safety during the months before delivery.

When the time nears for the baby to be delivered, the mother's birth pains become ever more severe and closer together. As the mother labors to deliver her child, the amniotic sac bursts and the baby is born. This birth is the watery birth to which Jesus was referring—not baptism!

Incidentally, I often hear folk describe the birth of a child as a "miracle." Nothing could be further from the truth! True, nothing is more awesome and beautiful than to witness the birth of a baby, but a baby is born as a result of natural laws created and instilled by our heavenly creator/ God! The only thing miraculous about a baby is that its life begins at conception!

Today evolutionists attempt to explain the origin of life as a simple, accidental chemical process. Even so, the insurmountable problem with an evolutionary explanation for the origin of life is the inability to explain how first life began. Because observation of all living species clearly demonstrates that only life can beget life, the source of all life is far beyond scientific explanation. Only one plausible explanation can be made for the origin of life: God! God created all life forms and instilled the laws of propagation to provide perpetuity of all life forms.

When a baby is born, it is born into a family, even if there has been no marriage ceremony; even if the husband is unknown or has deserted the mother, it still takes two—a man and a woman—to conceive a baby. Thus, when that baby is born, it has a physical father and a physical mother.

Jesus has pointed out that in order to become a conscious life on planet earth, one must experience a physical birth. No other way exists for a child to enter into this world.

Likewise, just as one must have a physical birth in order to see and experience this life, one must also have a spiritual birth in order to see and enjoy the spiritual dimension of life. Notice that when Jesus said one must be born of the flesh and of the Spirit, the word "Spirit" is capitalized. That is because Jesus was referring to the Holy Spirit. God is a triune being; He is God the Father, Jesus the Son, and the Holy Spirit. The Holy Spirit, therefore, is the source and the means of the second birth, the birth of the Spirit of which Jesus spoke.

Chapter IV
Once Born, One Cannot Be Unborn

It is a simple fact that no one who has been born on earth can ever be unborn. Several years ago, I was asked to visit a prisoner in the McAlester State Prison, who was condemned to die in the electric chair; in fact, he did die by electrocution a few weeks later.

This man, whom I shall call Max, had lived a life of crime. He finally killed a policeman and was sentenced to death. I vividly recall our visit and his cold and indifferent attitude toward the Christian faith.

Since then, I have thought of this man many times as being a perfect illustration of the fact that relationships are forever. This man had lived a life of crime; as a result, he had brought shame and reproach to the family name. No doubt he had gone by many different names; perhaps even his family had disowned him, but nothing in this world or the world to come could ever alter the fact Max was still his father's son. His father's blood still coursed through his veins. Relationships are forever!

Many have encountered such inescapable, insufferable misery that they wished they could die. Just a few days ago,

I visited a great Christian lady whom I pastored for eleven years. She was, without question, one of the most Christ-like persons I have ever known and had faithfully taught a ladies' Sunday school class for many years. In our conversation, she told me how she wished she could die and go on to be with the Lord and be reunited with her beloved husband who had preceded her in death not long before. Nonetheless, she has to wait on the "appointed time." As we have learned from the Word in Hebrews: "…it is appointed unto men once to die. But, after this, the judgment" (9:27).

Although one cannot be unborn, one can take his or her own life. In the interval from 1979 to 1996, a total of 535,890 deaths in the USA were diagnosed and reported as suicides.[2]

It is an inescapable and irrefutable fact that one who has been born into this world can never be unborn. Likewise, in every respect, one who has been born spiritually can never be unborn. The Bible continuously and consistently refers to "His people" as "His children." This is not a New Testament teaching only. In fact, from the very beginning of the biblical story, the people of Israel were referred to as the children of God!

When God's people came to Mt. Sinai after being delivered from Egyptian bondage, God used Moses to deliver the Ten Commandments, which presented the basic laws they were to live by and obey. The book of Leviticus is a broader, detailed, presentation of the requirements which God demands His children observe.

---

2   www.fathersforlife.org. Accessed online March 20, 2012.

Many people visualize almighty God as someone who is eager to punish us when we do things we know we ought not. I remember as a small boy growing up on a farm in southeastern Oklahoma, my concept of God was that everywhere I went God's big, black, heavy booted foot was hovering just over my head, and if I did anything I wasn't supposed to do, that big, heavy, booted foot was going to come down and stomp me out of existence.

As I grew older and developed a broader understanding of God's attitude toward His children, I visualized that when I sinned against my heavenly Father, I saw tears flowing down His cheeks. When we sin against our heavenly father, it breaks His heart. Thankfully, our loving Father is eager and ready to forgive our sins if only we repent and ask Him.

Chapter 26 of Leviticus presents the magnificent blessings of obedience and the horrible consequences of disobedience. God warns His people that disobeying His commandments can result in severe punishment. In verse 44, however, a compassionate heavenly Father states, "Yet for all that, when they are in the land of their enemies, I will not cast them away, nor shall I abhor them, *to utterly destroy them and break my covenant with them* for I am the Lord their God." [Emphasis added.]

Deuteronomy 4:30-31 also states, "When you are in distress, and all these things come upon you in the latter days, when you turn to the Lord your God and obey his voice (for the Lord your God is a merciful God), He will not forsake you nor destroy you, nor forget the covenant of your fathers which He swore to them."

Judges 2:1 further states, "Then the angel of the Lord came up from Gilgal to Bochim, and said, "I led you up from Egypt and brought you to the land of which I swore to your fathers; and I said, I will never break my covenant with you."

King David committed terrible sins of pride, covetousness, adultery, and murder. Did David utterly lose his relationship with God? Even David felt he had sinned so grievously that God could never forgive such heinous deeds. In spite of his fear, when David cried out in true repentance, God not only forgave all his sin but also cleaned him up and used him to write Holy Scripture.

In the New Testament, Jesus said in John 6:37, "All that the Father gives me will come to me, and the one who comes to Me, I *will in no wise cast out.*" [Emphasis added.] We could paraphrase this passage to read, "Under no circumstances will I cast away one who comes to me." We are often disobedient. Sometimes we sin terrible sins, but God never casts us out. He may punish us, but he will never cast us away. What a wonderful, eternal relationship we have with our heavenly Father.

Perhaps no greater passage of Scripture than that of Romans 11:29 more clearly describes our unbreakable relationship with our Father God, Jesus Christ, and Holy Spirit: "For the gifts and the calling of God are irrevocable."

For many years, this verse as presented in the old King James version never reached out and grabbed me. In the original King James version, we read, "For the gifts and calling of God are without repentance." When I read this verse in any of the newer translations, the revelation was dynamic. One can be a doctor but mess up and lose his license. One can be a lawyer but mess up and lose his license. One can be a beautician but mess up and lose her license; in fact, all professionals can mess up so badly they can loses their licensees.

Most Christians feel that their chances of making it to Heaven are based solely on whether or not their good deeds outweigh their evil deeds. On the contrary, we are now in the age of grace. As proof, let's look at Romans 3:19-28:

> Now we know that whatever the law says, it says to those who are under the law, that every mouth may be stopped and all the world may be guilty before God. Therefore, by the deeds of the law, no flesh will be justified in His sight, for by the law is the knowledge of sin. *But now the righteousness of God apart from the law is revealed,* being witnessed by the Law and the Prophets, even the righteousness of God through faith in Jesus Christ, to all and on all who believe. For there is no difference; for all have sinned and fall short of the glory of God, being *justified freely by His grace* through the redemption that is in Christ Jesus whom God set forth as a propitiation by his blood, through faith, to demonstrate His righteousness, because in His forbearance God has passed over the sins that were previously committed...*therefore we conclude that a man is justified by faith apart from the deeds of the law.* [Emphasis added.]

W. A. Chriswell writes in his *Baptist Study Bible* that "Justification" is perhaps the most crucial concept in Romans. Together with concepts such as sanctification, regeneration, reconciliation, and glorification, justification is one of the brilliant hues of God's salvation as reflected through the prism of God's word. Whereas regeneration describes the inner change brought to the child of God through faith, justification is a legal term designed to picture the believer's new status before God. As a result of His redemption in Christ, man is provided through grace, a righteous standing before God. As a sinner, man is guilty and must be condemned; however, the vicarious death of Jesus on the cross paid the penalty of sin, and on that basis God declares men of faith to be justified, i.e., to be treated as though innocent." [3] [Emphasis added.]

I have often said that God has forgiven all our sins *just as if we'd* never sinned at all.

Many Christians have great difficulty accepting the biblical teaching that it is not our righteousness that is going to get us to Heaven, but, the righteousness of Jesus Christ! A careful study of the foregoing quote from Criswell should help a great deal to clarify one's understanding of this subject.

While it is true that once one has been born into God's family, he cannot be unborn, and his sins are already covered through the shed blood of Christ, it is imperative to note that this fact is in no way a license to sin. In a later chapter, we will deal with the issue of God's punishment for our sins.

---

3   W.A. Crisswell. *Baptist Study Bible*, (Nashville: Thomas Nelson)p 1603.

Chapter V
Family Relationships

One enters into this world only by means of a natural [*physical*] birth. Even if the child born is a product of artificial insemination, the infant still has a father and a mother. This child is a recipient of inherited traits and characteristics from both its father and mother.

Everyone born into this world is born into a family comprised of at least a father and mother. When my father was born in 1902, he was born into a family that had fourteen children.

The central message of this book is to present biblical truths informing us that when we experience the second [*spiritual*] birth Jesus was telling us about in the third chapter of John, we are born *spiritually* into the family of God. The truth is that all who experience the second birth, living or dead, are brothers and sisters in Christ. This is not simply an illustration, or a parable, or a simile, but is a veritable fact. This is evidenced by the "ties that bind" loving relationships Christians develop for one another.

I have had the privilege of associating with Christian groups in several foreign countries,. In every instance I experienced a warm, loving sense of relationship with them.

On one mission trip to Hong Kong, I established a wonderful relationship with a young medical student with whom I corresponded for several years.

It is both informative and enlightening to take note of the fact that no where in Holy Scriptures is any reference to anyone in this world who attains full spiritual maturity! We remain the children of God in this world and in the world to come. No doubt one reason for our remaining as children is to emphasize that we have a "whole lot of growing up" to do.

Our Loving Father

With our limited, finite minds, the infinite depth of God's love for every soul He created is impossible for us to comprehend. Even those in infamy, whom we think would be impossible for even God to love, He loves them also. It is difficult for us to comprehend how anyone could love someone like Adolph Hitler or Joseph Stalin, but the Bible assures us that He does indeed.

Perhaps no greater Scripture illuminates our understanding of God's infinite, indestructible love than that of Psalm 139:13-18: ...

> you formed my inward parts; you covered me in
> my mother's womb. I will praise You, for I am
> fearfully and wonderfully made. Marvelous are
> Your works, and that my soul knows very well.
> My frame was not hidden from you, when I was
> made in secret, and skillfully wrought in the lower

parts of the earth. Your eyes saw my substance, being yet unformed, and in Your book they were all written, the days fashioned for me, when as yet there were none of them. How precious also are your thoughts to me, O God! How great is the sum of them! If I should count them, they would be more in number than the sand; When I awake, I am still with You.

We are not the product of mass production. We were personally created by our ever-loving God, who created the entire universe and everything that is in it. God had a special reason and purpose in creating us. We are so precious to Him, and none other in the world can take our place. God wants us! God had a special purpose for creating each one of us; furthermore, I believe He has gifted every believer with special abilities that enable us to do great things for the cause of Jesus Christ.

W. A. Criswell had this to say concerning this passage from Psalm 139:

This passage extols God for his marvelous work in human creation and constitutes the most important periscope in Scripture on one's self image. God prescribed the custom design for each individual (vv. 14-16) to equip one for achievement and purpose. The Creator never finishes but continues to edify and build up the creation, because, as the Creator, He receives glory/or dishonor according to the fruits of His creation (Matthew 5:16).

The importance of self-image is threefold: (1) to realize one's own potential, (2) to relate to others, one must develop his own testimony, (3) to relate to God, one must honor Him as the Creator/ Designer.[4]

This passage in Psalms 119 dramatically informs us how God created each of us according to a specific plan and purpose He had for each of us. Someone once pointed out that even before God made you or me, He knew every sin we would commit and yet He made us anyway. What an awesome, loving God.

It must be emphasized that while our Creator God created every human being that has been born on this planet Earth, He is NOT the Father of every one whom He created. God is the Father ONLY of His children who have been born spiritually into His kingdom and into His family.

The Bible teaches us that all God's children on earth are brothers and sisters in Christ Jesus. We are the family of our heavenly Father. In the churches I have pastored, I have observed, and personally felt, that Christians in a church body often become closer in personal relationships with other members of the church than with many of their earthly family relatives. Such relationships are precisely what the biblical mandate for Christian is meant to be.

4   Ibid, p.837

Chapter VI
Family Discipline

Children of God do sin. Some denominations insist their people live without sinning against God. How wonderful that would be if it were indeed true. On the contrary, the Bible clearly tells us over and over that Christians do sin. As stated earlier, even the apostle Paul indicated he considered himself as chief of sinners.

I recall a number of years ago visiting with a member of one of the denominations that claim they live above sin. After a brief discussion on the subject, I could see that this young man considered the only sins that exist are the sins of commission. Yet, there are two divisions of sin; sins of commission and sins of omission.

I asked him the following question: "If you had a neighbor whom you knew had never professed faith in Jesus Christ, and year after year you did not witness your faith to him or even invited him to your church, would that be sin?" His response was "No!" When I asked why would it not be sinful, he replied, "That would only be displeasing God." I wanted to explain to my friend that anything we do that displeases God is sin!

Perhaps it would be judicious here to define what sin is. The most common definition of sin is "Missing the Mark." Such imagery depicts an archer who carefully aims at a distant target. Exercising all the strength he can muster, he draws the bowstring and arrow as far back as he possibly can, remains steady, and lets fly the arrow; but he always falls short of the target!

Some biblical historians have reported that in the time when the apostle Paul was a young, devoted Jewish student, the general belief was that if any one person on earth could live just one day only without sin, the Messiah would come. Try and try as they might, they failed every time they attempted to fulfill that dream.

The Bible tells us in Romans 3:10, "…there is none righteousness; no not one." Again, in Romans 3:23, we read, "For all have sinned and fall short of the glory of God."

Man is born with an innate proclivity to sin. Even the youngest, when asked if they spilled the milk, will almost certainly declare, "No! I didn't do it!"

This obviates the inherent sinful nature of human kind.

Parents are wise if, even at an early age, they teach their little ones that they will be punished for doing things they ought not do.

When we do things we know we ought not do, the Bible tells us our heavenly Father disciplines us.

Hebrews 12:5 clarifies the term:

> "And you have forgotten the exhortations which speak to you as to sons: My sons [*my children*]. Do not despise the chastening [*discipling*] of the Lord, nor be discouraged when you are rebuked by Him; *for whom the Lord loves, he chastens and scourges every son whom He receives.* If you endure chastisement, God deals with you as sons; for what son is there whom a father does not chasten? *But if you are without chastising, of which all [children of God] have become partakers, then you are illegitimate and NOT sons!"* [Emphasis added.]

What a startling revelation! If God does take us to the whipping post, it is proof positive that we are truly His children. Even so, if one continues to sin and God leaves him alone and doesn't chastise or scourge him, the Scripture says that person is not a born-again Christian. Many times I have said from the pulpit, "If you can do anything you want to do and get by with it, you are not a Christian, because God disciplines ALL His children.

Incidentally, the word "chastisement" refers to any form of mild, punitive measures, such as we had when our parents only gave us a slap on the wrist or a single slap to our bottom. On the other hand, the word "scourge" means any form of severe punishment God may have to use in order to cause us to turn from our sinful ways and be obedient to Him. Some scholars suggest the word "scourge" conjures the image of a hook being placed in one's jaws in order to turn him around.

Several years ago, I was preaching a revival in a small mission church in Fargo, North Dakota. One night I preached on the subject of our heavenly Father's discipline. As I concluded my message, I stated that God's Word tells us if any can go on sinning and God leaves them alone, they are not children of God. As the pastor led in a dismissal prayer, he prayed, "Oh, God, bring forth your discipline that we may know we have truly been saved."

I have said many times from the pulpit that if you can do anything you want to and God leaves you alone, you are not a child of His! He disciplines only His own!

The Bible tells us from beginning to end that when we sin, we must repent of our sins in order to avoid punishment and restore joyous relations with our Heavenly Father. Just as we do not reward our children for bad behavior, God never blesses disobedient children. On the other hand, when we admit our sin, God is quick to forgive us our sins and cleanse us from all unrighteousness.

Perhaps it needs to be said that if we think our all-wise, all-knowing God won't know how best to cause us to regret our sins, we are badly mistaken! God, being God, always knows perfectly how best to discipline His children in the most effective and productive ways.

Sadly, many born-again Christians believe they will lose their salvation if they commit grievous sins.

I recall an incident that occurred a long time ago. A lady, who was a member of a local holiness church, told me of an incident in which she had been involved that led to her and a neighbor meeting in the middle of a street, each one in the face of the other and screaming epitaphs at each other. My friend said, "Brother Cal, I got so angry at that lady, that had I died that very moment, I would have gone straight to Hell."

I tried to assure her that would not have happened, but I am quite sure it didn't register, for she blurted out, "If I believed what you Baptists believe, I would do anything I want to do."

I replied, "If you believe what Baptists believe, you would *not* do anything you want to do!"

God carries a big stick! I don't know about you, but I am scared to death of God! The Bible tells us that fear of God is the beginning of wisdom.

I do all I can to keep from committing sin for three reasons: First, and foremost, I want to please my loving Heavenly Father who continues to bless me and my family, faithfully and abundantly day after day, after day. Second, I have learned that nothing is of such value that it is worth the deep guilt and regret I feel until I have repented and obtain His forgiveness. Third, I have experienced God's chastisement and scourging. Take it from me, I know what I'm talking about. God does indeed know what punishment to mete out to make you regret your sins.

I believe that today so many born-again Christians have drifted so far away from God it would be difficult for them to ascertain their salvation. No doubt, most of these would have no assurance of their salvation either. Of all people, I believe these people are the most miserable.

I believe two spiritual conditions befall *every* backslidden child of God when we drift so far away from what we know we should be doing:

(1) I believe the first thing a backsliding Christian experiences is a loss of the sense of inner peace and assurance of his salvation.

(2) The Bible teaches us that our Heavenly Father cannot bless His children who are disobedient any more than earthly parents cannot reward their children for disobedience.

I believe it is true what Constantine said God has made us for Himself, and our hearts will know no peace until we rest in Him.

It is, therefore, impossible for any human being on earth to find true, abiding peace and happiness in this life without having a right relationship with our Creator/God! If one recognize he has sinned against God, I can assure you there will be no real abiding peace in his heart until confession and repentance has been offered up to God!

One of the greatest barriers standing in the way of many lost people, blocking them from coming to Jesus Christ, is the fact they see some of the terrible sins that we Christians commit. In their minds, they consider themselves as good as any of us who attend church because they see some of the terrible things we Christians do. What a terrible tragedy when we Christians display such weakness of character that we impede the possibilities of someone coming to Christ. How desperately careful we should be not to be stumbling blocks to anyone.

What unbelievers cannot comprehend is that Christians do sin. We do not become sinless when we receive our salvation. Just as was mentioned earlier, even the apostle Paul admitted he continued to commit grievous sins.

Although Christians do sin, the Bible teaches us over and over that God forgives His children of their sins because we have a Savior who took away the eternal penalty of our sin. I like the statement so often used: "I am a sinner saved by the grace of God."

Chapter VII
Our Heavenly Home

How life first began is the one question no one on earth can explain in scientific terminology. One might possibly propose some explanation for the formation of the first cell, but he could never explain how it became a living cell. One basic scientific, indisputable fact is that all life forms came into being from former life forms! The search for "missing links" in the evolutionary tree of life, are still missing simply because they do not exist.

Werhner Von Braun, the eminent rocket scientist, was Adolph Hitler's greatest scientist. At the end of World War II, he defected to America where he became America's leading scientist in space exploration. That research resulted in the development of a space machine that enabled us to put man on the moon.

Werhner Von Braun once said, "Life does not know extinction, it only knows transformation."

It is interesting to note that the first law of Thermodynamics teaches that matter, which is the "stuff" that constitutes all living and non-living substances, is never destroyed.

Water is a perfect example of this law. Water is H^2O; two parts hydrogen and one part oxygen. Boil water using equipment that enables the collection of hydrogen in one flask oxygen in another flask, until no water remains! Afterward, you can put the water back together again by transferring the hydrogen and the oxygen back into a single flask, and you will always have the exact same amount of water. This process could be repeated a million times and not one atom of water, nor one atom of hydrogen, would be destroyed. Again, matter is never destroyed! Matter can only be changed and moved around, but it can never be destroyed.

Life is like that. Although life is not a material substance, life is eternal, never ending. The Bible teaches that "God formed man of the dust (matter) of the ground and breathed into his nostrils the breath of life, and man became a living being" (Genesis 2:7).

When one dies, he *will* go on living. There are two eternal destinations, and every human being who has ever existed on earth is traveling toward one or the other of these ultimate destinies: heaven or hell! Ironically, the choice is all up to us. We WILL decide where we spend eternity. Will we live in an eternal Heaven or an eternal Hell?

Near Death Experiences

Many reports have been made of folk who, as they were dying, described in vivid detail some of the glorious episodes they were experiencing.

The apostle Paul informs us in 2 Corinthians 12:2-4, he personally was caught up into Heaven, and the things he saw were so utterly beautiful and indescribable that words did not exist to describe adequately the glorious wonders and sights that await us in our Heavenly home.

Many saints such as Stephen, in the fifth chapter of Acts, have described heavenly visions as they were dying. It seems, however, that in the last few years, a dramatic change has come about in the increase of the number of folk reporting phenomenal experiences of heavenly visions as they were dying. Could it be that for some reason God is presenting new and even greater revelations of the things that await us in Heaven?

It does seem that in very recent times we have heard more and more such stories from the lips of those who were dying. Some reported seeing indescribable sights and hearing incredibly beautiful music. Some told of seeing angels. Some even reported getting a glance of their home in Heaven!

One of the most prominent names in Southern Baptist history is the name of Dr. R. G. Lee, long-time pastor of Bellevue Baptist Church in Memphis, Tennessee.

Dr. Lee was widely known as one of the greatest preachers in the Southern Baptist Convention. He was frequently the guest speaker at conventions and conferences all over the United States. One sermon Dr. Lee was often asked to preach was his sermon on Heaven.

It was said that Dr. Lee was such a gifted orator he could almost draw pictures with words. His sermon on Heaven depicted the indescribable beauty and wonders that await the redeemed in our eternal home.

As Dr. Lee lay on his death bed, comatose and expected to expire any moment, suddenly, he sat up and was heard to mumble something about Heaven. When asked to repeat what he had said, he simply said, "And I didn't do it justice!" Immediately, he lay back down and drew his last breath. Beyond doubt, Dr. Lee was viewing the same indescribable beauty the apostle Paul had seen.

The most dramatic near-death experience I have ever read about is the story of a little boy, Colton Burpo. Colton, who was not quite four years old, had undergone an emergency appendectomy. Later he reported that, during the surgery, he had left his body and gone to Heaven.[5] In the weeks and months to follow, the family finally concluded that there was no other credible explanation for the amazing things Colton related than it truly must have happened just as Colton described.

For instance, one day he told his mother he had two sisters. His mother sought to correct him, explaining that he had only one sister. He insisted again and again. Finally, the mother asked why he insisted he had two sisters. In answer, he replied that when he was in Heaven, a little girl came up to him and said she was his little sister who had died in his mother's stomach. The mother was stunned beyond description, for suddenly she remembered she had had a miscarriage but had never told Colton anything about it. Other than the heavenly experience, Colton could never have known.

Another major earth-shaking revelation came after Colton reported he had seen and talked with his grandfather

---

5   Todd Burpo, *Heaven is For Real*,. (Nashville: Nelson, 2010).

in Heaven. His parents dug out several photos they had of grandfather and showed them, but Colton did not recognize any of them.

Finally, they recalled that Colton had talked about how young everybody was in Heaven and that no one wore eyeglasses. Immediately, the family searched until they had found a photo of grandfather at a much earlier age. When shown the photo and asked who this was, without hesitation, Colton said it was his grandfather.

Another remarkable story about a child who walked and talked with God is the book, *Akiane*.[6] Akiane, also only four years old, one day announced to her mother that she had talked with God. Her atheistic parents tried to dismiss the ongoing stories Akiane told about her experiences with God. Simultaneously, Akiane began to show incredible talent in art. She explained that when she was with God, He taught her to paint. Akiana's artistic talent, even at four-to-six years of age, exhibited incredible, ingenious capabilities. One painting she created at age six sold for $10,000. Later, her painting would draw up to $100,000.

One picture that has brought international acclaim is her painting of Jesus. This painting was based on her personal visits with Jesus, and the art work became an overnight success.

In the meantime, Colton Burpo had told his parents that when he went to Heaven, he saw Jesus and even sat on His lap. His parents showed him various paintings of Jesus, but when asked to identify them, Colton explained he did not know.

---

6   Akiane and Foreli Kramarik, *Akiane*, (Nashville: Nelson, 2006).

When the Burpo family heard of the painting of Jesus by Arkiane, they obtained a copy, and when they showed it to Colton, he immediately identified it as Jesus.

When one considers the mysterious phenomena associated with these two small children as they reported on their visits with Jesus and angels, and many other seemingly incredible experiences, no explanation can be made other than they were indeed blessed by miraculous revelations of our heavenly Father and His eternal kingdom in Heaven..

What Can We Know About Heaven?

When my wife of fifty years died almost four years ago, I desperately wanted to know all I could learn about Heaven, for I suddenly realized that although I was a long-time pastor with a doctorate from seminary, I knew precious little about Heaven.

I began calling my learned friends and quickly found out they didn't know any more than I did.

At that time, I determined to do an in-depth study on the subject of Heaven. Since I know the Bible is the only source of irrefutable truths, I pored over all the Scripture passages I could find in relation to Heaven.

Amazed at the abundance of information available in the Bible, I quickly learned much of that information is veiled in the background of major biblical events and can be easily overlooked.

For instance, the story of the transfiguration of Jesus, as told by Matthew, Mark and Luke, describes the miraculous events that took place on a high mountain, probably in a remote location in northern Israel.

The disciples accompanying Jesus were Peter, James, and John. While Jesus prayed, the disciples fell asleep. Suddenly, they were awakened and startled by a strange, inexplicable phenomenon occurring before their eyes. Jesus' body was radiating in His "shekinah" glory—a glory that was more brilliant than the sun.

While it is only natural for us to focus on the spectacular change in Jesus' body, much more can be gleamed from this setting. For instance, Peter, James, and John are suddenly aware that Jesus is talking with two gentlemen, Moses and Elijah, both of whom had gone to Heaven centuries before. How could the disciples have recognized Moses and Elijah? They had no idea what they looked like. Yet they did know them without an introduction from Jesus.

Moses had died on a mountain and God Himself had hidden his body. Moses had now been in Heaven for several hundred years.

Elijah was an individual who had not died. The Bible reports that he was caught up bodily in a whirlwind and taken to Heaven. Both of these spiritual giants had obviously been living in Heaven for hundreds of years.

One of the most important lessons we learn from this event is BOTH MOSES AND ELIJAH HAD BODIES! They certainly were not disembodied spirits floating around as many believe we shall be when we get to Heaven. Moses and Elijah had bodies! And so will we!

One passage of Scripture that seems to confirm the fact we will have bodies is found in Revelation 6:9-11. This passage describes the great number of martyrs who are seen here under the altar. Verse 11 reads, "...white robes were given unto every one of them." Robes are not for disembodied spirits; robes are for bodies.

The Bible tells us that there are terrestrial (earthly) bodies and there are celestial (heavenly) bodies (1 Corinthians 15:40). No one can tell us what kind of material our bodies will exhibit, but we will have bodies! Eventually, at the great resurrection, we will get our earthly bodies back, and they will be perfect bodies, totally devoid of any sin curse. These shall then be our bodies throughout eternity.

In the midst of my studies on Heaven, I came to know I had to write a book to present some of the marvelous things I learned which brought such profound peace and comfort to my suffering soul. That book, entitled *Glimpses of Heaven: A Biblical Study on Heaven*,[7] is available from major book stores and online book sellers such as Amazon.com.

Our Perfect Bodies

Young Colton reported in *Heaven Is for Real,* there will be no eyeglasses in Heaven. Think of it! There will be no missing parts. There will be no infirmities. There will be no blindness, no hearing aids, no dentures, no wheelchairs. All in Heaven are going to be perfect physical specimens.

Quadriplegics and paraplegics will walk; blind folk will see with perfect vision. I also believe no "uglies" will be in Heaven. Everyone will be beautiful.

Good evidence suggests that we are all going to be a lot smarter in Heaven than we are here. Scientists are convinced that we, today, normally use less than ten percent

---

7   Cal Hunter, *Glimpses of Heaven: A Biblical Study on Heaven*, (Star Publish LLC, 2009).

of our intelligence. No doubt this is also a part of the sin curse, and when we get to Heaven and the sin curse is removed, we shall be able to use one hundred percent of our intelligence. What will it be like if we are all ninety percent smarter in Heaven than we are here on earth?

What Age Will We Appear To Be?

Over the years, much discussion has been on what age we will appear to be in Heaven. Thomas Aquinas (1225 - 1274) was the first to suggest that since Jesus died at the age of thirty-three years, we also will likely present that same age when we get to Heaven.

Science has also given us reason to believe we will appear to be somewhere around that age when we get to Heaven. Scientific studies have determined that our DNA peaks our physical fitness and mental acuity somewhere around thirty years of age. After that it's all downhill. Slowly but steadily, as we age, we find we can do less work, have more dental and physical ailments, learn more slowly, suffer vision impairment and develop memory loss. This is a result of the sin curse which ultimately brings about death!

When the sin curse is removed when we get to Heaven, we shall have perfect bodies and minds for all of eternity.

Why do you suppose that some of those closest to Jesus were unable to recognize Him after His resurrection? Until Jesus' death, He bore the same sin cursed fleshly body that you and I have; however, when Jesus returned from His visit to Paradise, He took on his *new* body—His *resurrected* body, a body that bore no marks of the sin curse. His body was a perfect body. As a result, this body was different in many aspects, for He was able now to go through walls without opening doors.

Luke records the event in which the disciples, in fear of the Jews, were assembled behind *locked* doors when suddenly Jesus stood in their midst (Luke 24:36). No knock had sounded at the door and no one had opened the door, but suddenly Jesus was standing in their very midst.

I cannot help but believe that the body Jesus bore while on earth came to bear many harsh marks as a result of the many long hours of hard work in the hot, windy, Mediterranean climate. Such heat and labor could have produced some early marks of aging, even at his thirty-three years when He died.

I sincerely believe that because Jesus' resurrected body caused Him to look much younger than he had appeared before His death, His followers did not readily recognize Him.

An interesting note here is that for the duration of the time Jesus spent on this earth after His resurrection, He modeled the body we shall have when we, too, are resurrected—the perfect bodies we shall have for all eternity.

We Shall See God

No one has ever attempted to suggest what God will be like. While the Bible informs us that we are made in His image, this does not necessarily mean that God will look like us. No one can know that. Colton once told his parents that God is awfully big!

Can you imagine standing before an all-wise, all-knowing, all- powerful God who made everything that exists? We know He knows everything about us, every sin we have committed! It sounds so awesome, so frightening, and so disturbing, but when we remember the Bible teaches us that God loves us with such a pure, sweet, boundless, and indestructible love, we will have no cause for fear and trepidation. He is our heavenly Father. Besides that, the Bible informs us that when God forgives our sins, He even forgets them (Psalms 103:12).

We shall see Jesus, who loved us so much He gave Himself to die the cruelest death ever devised by man (crucifixion) in order to remove the penalty for all our sin.

We shall see the scars on His head left by the crown of thorns. We shall see the scar on his side where the spear pierced his heart. Yes, those scars will still be there even though our scars will all be gone.

You will no doubt remember the event in which Jesus invited Thomas to examine the scars in His hands, and to thrust his finger into the hole in His side (John 20:27). Those scars will forever remind us of the pain and suffering Jesus endured for our redemption.

Indescribable Beauty and Music

Two of the most common subjects that folk report in their dying moments are the indescribable beauty of Heaven, and the incredibly beautiful music they hear. Some even report they see Jesus or angels.

One pastor I personally know told me how he had sat by the bedside of an old gentleman who was dying, and suddenly the gentleman asked, "Can't you hear the singing?" In a moment he said again, "How beautiful the singing is," and then he died.

Another well-known pastor and friend of mine was Alvin McConelI. Alvin was pastor of First Baptist Church, Lindsey, Oklahoma, for a great number of years. His wife told me that as he lay dying, he kept trying to get up.

With each effort, his son pleaded, "Stay in bed, Dad."

Each time, Alvin replied, "I've got to get up."

His son asked, "Why do you have to get up?"

Alvin replied, "You ought to see my home!" A short time later he was gone.

A famous preacher once said if we had any idea how close and how real God is to us this very minute, we might be scared to death. On the other hand, if we knew how beautiful and wonderful Heaven is, we would be tempted to commit suicide in our hurry to get there.

A Great Reunion

One of the greatest promises the Scriptures offer us is that when we get to Heaven, we shall be reunited with all our loved ones who have already gone to be with the Lord. We all have a great many loved ones we long to see and we shall. Not only shall we be able to sit down with our loved ones whom we have longed so long to see, but also we shall be privileged to sit down and visit with some of the greatest souls who ever existed. Can you imagine sitting down with folk such as the Old Testament patriarchs whom we have studied and admired, or with folk such as Noah, David,

Peter, James, John, and the apostle Paul? What a blessing to realize we will have all eternity for such visits.

I frankly confess I am really getting anxious to see the glorious sights of Heaven, and to see my Heavenly Father, and my Savior Jesus Christ. I also hunger deeply to see all my beloved relatives and friends who have already gone there.

In addition, have you ever realized that we will be able to sit down with many of our ancestors—most of whom we never knew existed? What a wonderful life Heaven will offer us.

Chapter VIII
Can It Possibly Be True?

I have never heard of a race of people who existed in our world, regardless of how primitive or uncivilized they may have been, who did not have a concept of an all-powerful, all-knowing, divine being whom they worshiped. Until somewhere around the eighteenth century, few atheists, if any at all, were in the world.

In the latter part of the nineteenth century, a German philosopher by the name of Friedrich Nietzsche (1844-1900), published a book titled, *God Is Dead!* Since that time, a meteoric increase in the number of self- proclaimed atheists abounded. About eighty-five percent of people in America still believe in God, but the number of non-believers is steadily growing.

An interesting note I have observed from my studies is that the growth of atheism paralleled the growth of education. As he advances in his education and knowledge, man has a tendency to "lean on his own understanding." A perfect example of this "understanding" is the growth of Humanism, a philosophy currently embraced by most colleges and universities, academicians, and scientists.

Essentially, Humanism is the philosophy which states God does not exist. We (mankind) are the only God we will ever have. It's up to us to usher in our utopia.

Instead of utopia, that philosophy has ushered in world-wide disintegration of every major human institution. Our economic, executive, legislative, judicial, and educational systems are in total disarray. Every facet of our existence is mired in confusion and perplexity.

It is no wonder that Jesus said in Luke 18:8, "...when the Son of Man comes, will He really find faith on the earth?"

One of the major reasons that so many have been drawn away from our Christian faith is a result of the teaching of the theory of evolution as scientific fact. Nothing could be further from the truth. In all of history, never, ever, has one single tenet of evolutionary teaching been proven scientifically. On the other hand, never, ever, has a single tenet of biblical teaching been proven in a court of law to be false. Evolution is still a theory, but is being presented as scientific fact.

Because so many tenets of evolution are being embraced by Christian scholars and leaders, some of the most basic scriptural facts are being questioned and rejected because they do not harmonize with evolutionary teaching.

For instance, not only have many Christian scholars come to accept the theory that life existed millions of years before Adam and Eve were created, but also that many giant animals lived and died before Adam and Eve's time. I would argue that even if animals had existed millions of years before Adam and Eve, they could not have died until

Adam and Eve sinned and the sin curse that included death was pronounced on mankind and all other life forms. Until Adam and Eve sinned, death did not exist!

Many Christian teachers and leaders are proposing that a time-gap of millions of years exists between Genesis 1:1 and Genesis 1:2. They also reject the idea of a six-day creation. Since not one error has ever been proven in the Bible, I ask, "Why would the Bible be wrong in only this one recording? It is my opinion that we either accept all that the Bible teaches or we accept none.

In my opinion, an abundance of faith is required to believe the first living cell on earth was accidentally produced when an accumulation of certain elements mysteriously came together in primordial soup and suddenly a stroke of lightning created the first living cell on earth. Subsequently, evolutionists argue all life forms on planet earth evolved from that one cell to bring in every living creature on earth. It takes more faith to believe that explanation than to accept the belief that life was created by an all-wise, all-powerful Creator. Life cannot be explained; it can only be observed.

Several years ago, I wrote a book on the evidence of intelligent design in human physiology.[8] In this book, I presented some of the inexplicably complex structures in the human body and explained how their functions work together harmoniously to keep our bodies on an "even keel."

---

8 Cal Hunter, *Evidence of Intelligent Design in Human Physiology*, (Star Publish, LLC: 2007)

The exceedingly, complex functions of such systems as our brains, our nervous system, our circulatory system, our digestive system, our immune system, and all the other systems in our bodies, present weighty evidence for an Intelligent Designer/Creator.

Our human bodies present more evidence for a creator than any other aspect of our existence. It is within man's anatomy and physiology that we see the handiwork of God more clearly than anywhere else. If one had only the evidence presented in one single cell, that information would be sufficient to present irrefutable evidence of a Creator. For instance, in each cell of our bodies, information within our DNA is sufficient to reproduce every cell in the human body! To believe that is the result of millions of years of slow, non-directed, random changes is, in my opinion, ludicrous.

I have been told that a certain Ivy League university professor once said that there are only two plausible explanations for our existence: evolution and creation. Of the two, he pointed out, the most plausible explanation is creation, "but," he added, "that is not acceptable."

Sir Fred Hoyle (1915–2001), England's most beloved scientist, mathematician, and astronomer, was a firm believer in evolutionary teaching. He decided he would devote several years of study to obtain enough scientific evidence to prove once and for all time the biblical account of creation is only a myth.

At the conclusion of his research, Sir Hoyle was asked what he believed the odds are that evolution offers a credible explanation for the origin of life.

Sir Hoyle replied by saying the odds that life began by an evolutionary process is one in $10^{40,000}$. Since scientists have estimated there are approximately one in 10^{80} number of atoms in our entire galaxy, Sir Hoyle was expressing in the language he knew best: mathematics, that it is entirely impossible for life to have evolved.

From his research, he determined it would be easier to visit a distant planet in our galaxy to find one specific atom!

Sir Hoyle went on to explain it would be easier for a tornado to enter the front gate of a large salvage yard and assemble a Boeing 747 airplane in flight as it exited the rear entrance.[9]

Although Sir Fred Hoyle sought to prove by his research that evolution is fact and creation is myth, his conclusion proved just the opposite is true. Life was indeed created by an all-wise, all-mighty Creator.

Many years ago, General Lew Wallace (1827–1905), United States Army General, declared that when he retired he was going to move to Europe where he would devote several years to find the information he would need to prove, once and for all time, that the Christian Bible is untrue. He later reported that after approximately two years of study, he found himself on his knees calling out to God to save him. He then wrote the book, *Ben Hur*, in an attempt to prove just the opposite: the Bible is both true and truly trustworthy.

When one considers the biblical accounts of Heaven, the many testimonies of prominent saints who reported

---

9 Wikipedia, free online encyclopedia. Accessed June 2, 2012.

great visions of Heaven as they were dying, and of the abundant information that assures us we are not here by accident, we learn we were created for life on earth and ultimately to be with our Lord Jesus Christ when we, too, leave this earthly abode.

We must remember, "The Lord is not slack concerning his promises, as some count slackness, but is longsuffering toward us, not willing that any should perish but that all should come to repentance" (Peter 3:9).

The growing rejection of biblical teaching and increase in humanistic pursuits, have resulted in a steady, growing, unrelenting assault on the Christian religion in our beloved America.

America is the only nation in the world that was founded on Christian principles; not just biblical principles, but Christian principles. The constitution our founders adopted guarantees absolute freedom of all religions and restricts none. Christianity, however, is now under continual attacks by executive orders, by federal judges who legislate by decree, and by the liberal media who make no attempt to hide their animosity toward the Christian religion.

Every possible tactic is being used to rob us of our age-old Christian traditions, such as public prayer, display of Christian flags, crosses, Christmas trees, and Christian symbols on our money. Currently, even a move to remove the phrase "under God" from our pledge of allegiance is being promoted. It is so sad that the only country that was ever founded on true Christian principles is now a country that literally hates the Christian religion. The Bible reports that Jesus said in Matthew 10:22. "...you will be hated by all for my name's sake."

The Great Delusion

The Bible informs us that in the last days, men will be so consumed by their evil desires and pursuits that they will reject the truth and believe a lie.

2 Thessalonians9-12, informs us:

> The coming of the lawless one is according to the working of Satan, with all power, signs and lying wonders, and with all unrighteous deception among those who perish because they did not receive the love of the truth, that they might be saved. **And for this reason God will send them strong delusion, that they should believe the lie**, that they may all be condemned who did not believe the truth but had pleasure in unrighteousness. [Emphasis added.]

Some biblical scholars point out that the Bible's favorite term for Satan is "Deceiver," and warns if we are not careful we, too, may be deceived into rejecting the truths of God and embracing the lies of Satan.

While Satan is powerful, his power is limited. He is, nonetheless, a powerful and super-intelligent creature. A careful study of the last two hundred years will reveal Satan has succeeded in deceiving an inestimable number of people into rejecting biblical truths and embracing Satan's lies.

Since the 19th century, atheism has experienced meteoric growth, which has given birth to Humanism and reliance on evolutionary explanations for our existence.

Humanism is now embraced by the vast majority of educators, academicians, and scientists. Humanism teaches that God is not real. We, mankind, are the only God we will ever have. It's up to us to usher in utopia. It is not difficult to gauge what success such concepts have brought about. If you look closely, you will observe that every facet of our existence is rapidly eroding into a sea of confusion and perplexity.

It is interesting to note that Satan has developed a three-headed strategy to destroy man's reliance on biblical truths: Atheism, Humanism, and Evolution. To embrace any one of these teachings leads one to reject the truths of God and to believe delusionary lies of Satan.

In the concluding chapter of Joshua, 24:15, Joshua challenged his people with these words: "...if it seems evil to you to serve the Lord, choose for yourselves this day whom you will serve...but as for me and my house, we will serve the Lord."

Chapter IX
Making Sure Of One's Salvation

Someone once remarked that when we get to Heaven we are going to have three great surprises: First, we are going to be surprised that some people made it to Heaven. Second, we are going to be surprised that some people didn't make it to Heaven. Third, we are going to be surprised we made it!

We have placed much emphasis on the fact that it is absolutely vital that one experiences the second birth: the spiritual birth. Just as one must be born to see and enjoy this world, one must be born into it. Likewise, if we are to see and enjoy eternal life in Heaven when we die, we must experience the second birth Jesus spoke about in the third chapter of John.

Simply "turning over a new leaf" or making a firm resolution to live a better life will not save us.

Merely joining a church will not get us to Heaven. Church membership is great and profitable; but we should be a Christian before we join a church.

Likewise, going forward during an invitation and taking the preacher's hand, in itself, will not save us.

Uniquely, salvation is both one of the easiest things on earth to do and, at the same time, the most difficult thing on earth to do. It is the easiest thing on earth to do because all we have to do is believe in Jesus and ask Him to forgive us of our sins and save our eternal soul. It is also one of the most difficult things on earth for us to do because we have to come to Jesus in total surrender of our lives to Him.

I have often heard preachers say something to the effect that "You have taken Jesus as your Savior; now make Him your Lord." That statement bothers me. I am not sure that when one comes to Jesus for salvation he can be saved, unless in that moment he is totally surrendered to the Lord.

Jesus is Lord! That is why at that moment we must be totally surrendered to Him in order to receive the second birth—the spiritual birth which we refer to as "born again." That is precisely what happens at the moment of our salvation. We are born spiritually into God's family.

In no way am I suggesting we must live every moment of our lives in that degree of surrender, although we should. In fact, that should be the supreme goal of every born-again Christian. Unfortunately, we are not capable of perfection, and Jesus understands. He knows when we are trying and He forgives us of our failures.

Unfortunately, the truth is we often sell Jesus out in our lives by doing what we want, not what Jesus wants. That is why we must constantly strive to make Him Lord of our lives, and when we fail, we must ask for His forgiveness, trusting in His forgiving nature.

Cal Hunter

In the many years of my ministry, I have led many to pray that simple prayer of confession and acceptance of Jesus as Lord. Many times I have said, "If you really meant everything you said in that prayer, I would throw this Bible away and never preach another sermon if I did not believe that He has indeed saved you."

In the eighth chapter of Acts, verses 26-40, the writer tells about Phillip, who encounters an Ethiopian eunuch sitting in his chariot reading the Bible. Phillip asked if he understood what he was reading. When the Ethiopian confessed he needed some help in understanding the Scriptures, verse 35-40 tells us:

> Then Phillip opened his mouth, and beginning
> at this scripture, preached Jesus to him. Now as
> they went down the road, they came to some water.
> And the eunuch said, 'See, here is water. What
> hinders me from being baptized?' Then Phillip said,
> *'If you believe with all your heart, you may.'* And he
> answered and said, 'I believe that Jesus Christ is the
> Son of God.' So he commanded the chariot to stand
> still. And both Phillip and the eunuch went down into
> the water, and he baptized him. [Emphasis added.]

Many people report that they know they have been saved, but still experience frequent periods of doubt. I believe all Christians experience some degree of doubt from time to time. I know I have. Why do Christians doubt their salvation?

Charles Haddon Spurgeon explained that doubting is proof of salvation. It is the soul reaching out for confirmation.

Bob Catlett, my "father in the ministry," once explained to me that you can't doubt what you know you don't have! You know!

Hyman Appleman, noted Christian Jewish evangelist, said, "We doubt because our faith is not yet made perfect."

Walter K. Ayres, noted evangelist, suggested two kinds of folk call themselves Christian: those who say they never doubt and those who say they often doubt. He went on to say that the more he learned the more he believed that those who often doubt are the real Christians, and those that never doubt are not Christians at all.

Hebrews 10:22-23, states, "Let us draw near with a true heart in full assurance of faith, having our hearts sprinkled from an evil conscience and our bodies washed with pure water. Let us hold fast the confession of our hope without wavering, for He who promised is faithful."

I have also come to the conclusion that some things do contribute to our doubt. Listed below are some of those things which I believe can contribute a great deal to our propensity to doubt:

1. We are not accustomed to having such good things happening to us.

2. I believe some think there must be more to it than what I have done.

3. The older we get the more we want to confirm our faith.

Fortunately, we can know that we are children of God, for many scriptures in the Bible clearly confirm whether or not we are truly born-again Christians.

Some of the greatest tests of one's salvation are the following:

1. Does something inside you seem to assure you that you are a child of God? The Bible tells us in Romans 8:16, "The Spirit Himself bears witness with our spirit that we are the children of God."

2. Does Christianity make sense to you? 1 Corinthians 2:14 reads, "…the natural man does not receive the things of the Spirit of God, for they are foolishness to him, nor can he know them because they are spiritually discerned."

3. Do you love and respect Christian people? 1 John 3:14 informs us: "We know we have passed from death to life, because we love the brethren. He who does now love his brother abides in death."

The greatest advice I have for everyone is to learn to trust the Bible implicitly. It is indeed the Word of God. Remember Paul's advise when he said, "…He who promised is faithful" (Hebrews 10:23).